Life Cycles

A Beetle's Life Cycle

by Jamie Rice

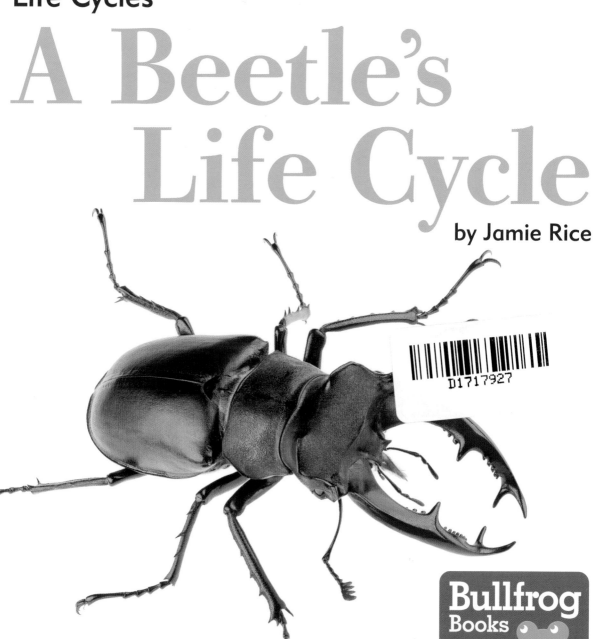

D1717927

Bullfrog Books

Ideas for Parents and Teachers

Bullfrog Books let children practice reading informational text at the earliest reading levels. Repetition, familiar words, and photo labels support early readers.

Before Reading

- Discuss the cover photo. What does it tell them?

- Look at the picture glossary together. Read and discuss the words.

Read the Book

- "Walk" through the book and look at the photos. Let the child ask questions. Point out the photo labels.

- Read the book to the child, or have him or her read independently.

After Reading

- Prompt the child to think more. Ask: Female beetles lay eggs. Can you name other animals that lay eggs?

Bullfrog Books are published by Jump!
5357 Penn Avenue South
Minneapolis, MN 55419
www.jumplibrary.com

Copyright © 2023 Jump! International copyright reserved in all countries. No part of this book may be reproduced in any form without written permission from the publisher.

Library of Congress Cataloging-in-Publication Data

Names: Rice, Jamie, author.
Title: A beetle's life cycle / by Jamie Rice.
Description: Bullfrog books.
Minneapolis, MN: Jump!, Inc., [2023]
Series: Life cycles | Includes index.
Audience: Ages 5–8
Identifiers: LCCN 2021048362 (print)
LCCN 2021048363 (ebook)
ISBN 9781636908199 (hardcover)
ISBN 9781636908205 (paperback)
ISBN 9781636908212 (ebook)
Subjects: LCSH: Beetles—Life cycles—Juvenile literature.
Classification: LCC QL576.2 .R527 2023 (print)
LCC QL576.2 (ebook)
DDC 595.76156—dc23/eng/20211004
LC record available at
https://lccn.loc.gov/2021048362
LC ebook record available at
https://lccn.loc.gov/2021048363

Editor: Eliza Leahy
Designer: Emma Bersie

Photo Credits: Protasov AN/Shutterstock, cover (top), 3, 5, 22t; Vinicius R. Souza/Shutterstock, cover (bottom); Anton Kozyrev/Shutterstock, 1; PHOTO FUN/Shutterstock, 4; Markus Schness/Dreamstime, 6–7, 23tr; gutaper/iStock, 8–9, 23bl; Arterra Picture Library/Alamy, 10–11, 23br; wonderisland/Shutterstock, 12, 23tm; Tanawat Palee/Shutterstock, 13; KSCHiLi/Shutterstock, 14–15, 22b, 23bm; JorgeOrtiz_1976/Shutterstock, 16; irin-k/Shutterstock, 17; Nastya/Dreamstime, 18–19; Stephane Bidouze/Shutterstock, 20–21; Afanasiev Andrii/Shutterstock, 22l, 22r; nadia_if/Shutterstock, 23tl; stella_photo/Shutterstock, 24.

Printed in the United States of America at Corporate Graphics in North Mankato, Minnesota.

Table of Contents

From Egg to Adult

It is spring.

A beetle finds a leaf.

egg

She lays eggs.

Another lays eggs on tree bark.

Days go by.

Larvae hatch.

larva

They grow.

They eat plants.

Munch!

They shed their skin.
They do this many times!

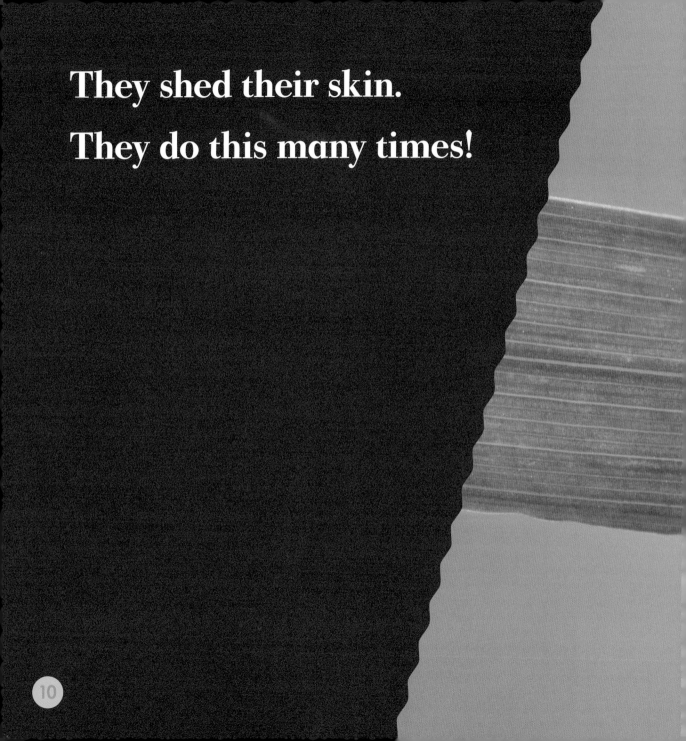

shed
skin

This one makes a hard case.

Now it is a pupa.

case

Some stay underground.

13

This pupa stays on a leaf.

Its case keeps it safe.

Inside, its body changes.

Ten days go by.
A beetle comes out!
It is an adult.

Adult beetles have two antennas.

They have six legs.

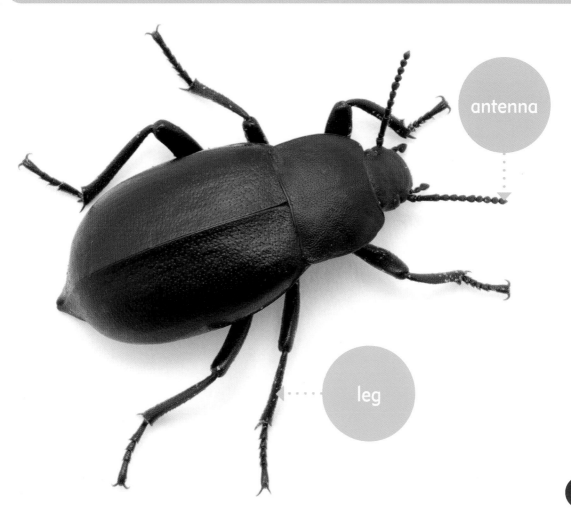

antenna

leg

wing

They have wings.
Two are hard.
Two are soft.
The soft wings
help them fly!

Soon they will
lay eggs, too!

Life Cycle of a Beetle

A beetle's life cycle has four stages. Take a look!

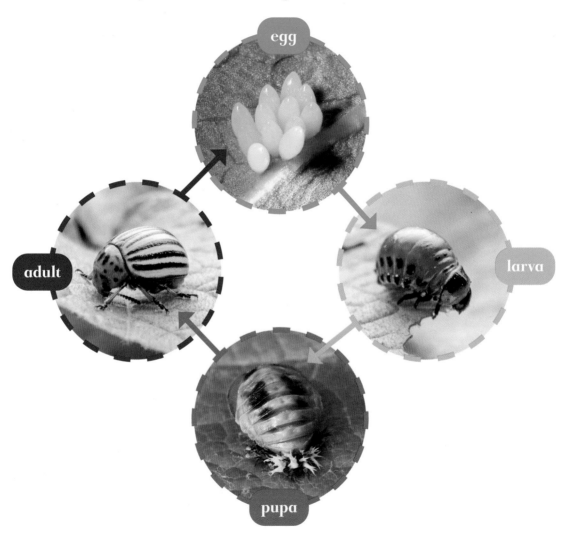

egg

larva

pupa

adult

Picture Glossary

bark
The tough outer covering on shrubs, trees, and other plants.

case
The outer covering of an object.

hatch
To break out of eggs.

larvae
Insects in the stage of growth between eggs and pupae.

pupa
An insect in the stage of growth between larva and adult.

shed
To lose, get rid of, or let something fall.

Index

To Learn More

Finding more information is as easy as 1, 2, 3.

❶ Go to www.factsurfer.com

❷ Enter "abeetle'slifecycle" into the search box.

❸ Choose your book to see a list of websites.